HAL•LEONARD

ESSENTIAL SONGS

PIANO

More of the 1960s

D1296341

ISBN-13: 978-1-4234-1801-6
ISBN-10: 1-4234-1801-8

HAL•LEONARD®
CORPORATION

7777 W. BLUEMOUND RD. P.O. BOX 13819 MILWAUKEE, WI 53213

Visit Hal Leonard Online at
www.halleonard.com

CONTENTS

204	It's My Party	Lesley Gore	1	1963
206	King of the Road	Roger Miller	4	1965
201	Last Train to Clarksville	The Monkees	1	1966
208	Leader of the Pack	The Shangri-Las	1	1964
212	Leaving on a Jet Plane	Peter, Paul & Mary	1	1969
220	Lightnin' Strikes	Lou Christie	1	1966
215	Limbo Rock	Chubby Checker	1	1960
224	Little Green Apples	Bobby Russell	1	1968
229	The Little Old Lady (From Pasadena)	Jan & Dean	3	1964
232	Louie, Louie	Kingsmen	2	1963
234	A Lover's Concerto	The Toys	2	1965
240	Magic Carpet Ride	Steppenwolf	3	1968
237	Mellow Yellow	Donovan	2	1966
244	Monday, Monday	The Mamas & The Papas	1	1966
254	My Boyfriend's Back	The Angels	1	1963
247	My Girl	The Temptations	1	1965
258	Na Na Hey Hey Kiss Him Goodbye	Steam	1	1969
260	(You Make Me Feel Like) A Natural Woman	Aretha Franklin	8	1967
265	Oh, Pretty Woman	Roy Orbison	1	1964
272	On Broadway	The Drifters	1	1963
274	One Fine Day	The Chiffons	5	1963
279	Peppermint Twist	Joey Dee and The Starliters	1	1961
282	Proud Mary	Creedence Clearwater Revival	2	1969
290	Puppy Love	Paul Anka	2	1960
294	Release Me	Engelbert Humperdinck	4	1967
287	Return to Sender	Elvis Presley	2	1962
296	Runaway	DelShannon	1	1961
300	San Francisco (Be Sure to Wear Some Flowers in Your Hair)	Scott McKenzie	4	1967
304	Sealed with a Kiss	Brian Hyland	3	1962
307	(Sittin' On) the Dock of the Bay	Otis Redding	1	1968
310	Somebody to Love	Jefferson Airplane	5	1967
317	Soul Man	Sam & Dave	2	1967
320	Spanish Eyes	Al Martino	15	1966
326	Spanish Flea	Herb Alpert	1	1965
330	Spinning Wheel	Blood, Sweat & Tears	2	1969
323	Strangers in the Night	Frank Sinatra	1	1966
334	Sugar, Sugar	The Archies	1	1969
338	Sukiyaki	Kyu Sakamoto	1	1963
343	Take Good Care of My Baby	Bobby Vee	1	1961
346	Teen Angel	Mark Dinning	1	1960
348	These Boots Are Made for Walkin'	Nancy Sinatra	1	1966
351	Those Were The Days	Mary Hopkin	2	1968
354	To Sir, with Love	Lulu	1	1967
360	The Twist	Chubby Checker	1	1960
362	Up On the Roof	The Drifters	5	1963
366	Up, up and Away	5th Dimension	7	1967
370	Walk on By	Dionne Warwick	6	1964
357	What the World Needs Now Is Love	Jackie DeShannon	7	1965
372	Wichita Lineman	Glen Campbell	3	1968
375	Wild Thing	The Troggs	1	1966
378	Wooly Bully	Sam the Sham & The Pharaohs	2	1965
380	Wouldn't It Be Nice	The Beach Boys	8	1966
390	Yellow Submarine	The Beatles	2	1966
394	You've Lost That Lovin' Feelin'	The Righteous Brothers	1	1965
383	You've Made Me So Very Happy	Blood, Sweat & Tears	2	1969

ABRAHAM, MARTIN AND JOHN

Words and Music by
RICHARD HOLLER

ALFIE
Theme from the Paramount Picture ALFIE

Words by HAL DAVID
Music by BURT BACHARACH

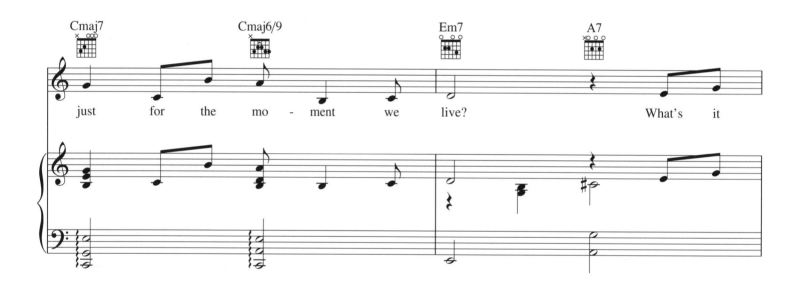

ALL ALONE AM I

English Lyric by ARTHUR ALTMAN
Original Lyric by JEAN IOANNIDIS
Music by M. HADJIDAKIS

lone - ly beat-ing of my heart. { No use in hold-ing oth - er
{ No oth - er voice can say the

hands, for I'd be hold-ing on - ly
words my heart must hear to ev - er

emp - ti - ness. No use in kiss-ing oth - er lips,
sing a - gain. The words you used to whis - per low,

for I'd be think-ing just of your ca - ress. }
no oth - er love can ev - er bring a - gain. } All a -

THE BIRDS AND THE BEES

Words and Music by
HERB NEWMAN

Moderately, with a beat

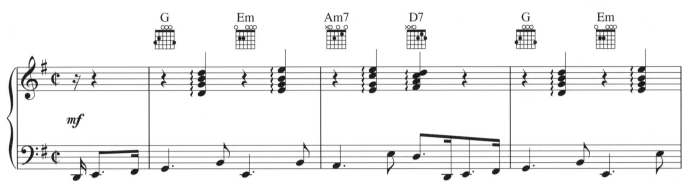

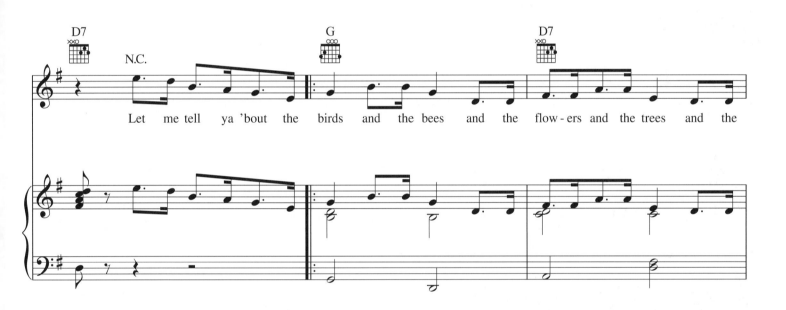

Let me tell ya 'bout the birds and the bees and the flow-ers and the trees and the

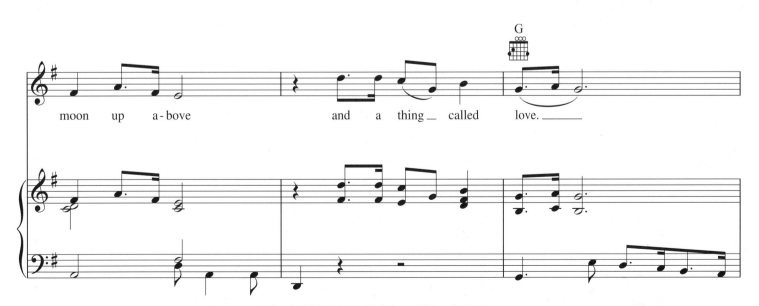

moon up a-bove and a thing __ called love. _____

ALONG COMES MARY

Words and Music by
TANDYN ALMER

Ev-'ry time I think that I'm ___ the on - ly one who's lone - ly, some-one ___
sire ___ is the fire ___ in ___ the eyes ___ of chicks whose sick-ness is the ___
morn-ing of the warn-ing's passed, ___ the gassed ___ and flac - cid kids are flung a -

___ calls ___ on me. ___ And ev-'ry now and then I spend my time
___ games ___ they play, ___ and when the mas-quer-ade is played, the neigh-bor folks ___
- cross ___ the stars. ___ The psy-cho-dra-mas and the trau-mas gone, the songs ___

(It's A)
BEAUTIFUL MORNING

Words and Music by FELIX CAVALIERE
and EDWARD BRIGATI, JR.

BEYOND THE SEA

Words and Music by CHARLES TRENET,
ALBERT LASRY and JACK LAWRENCE

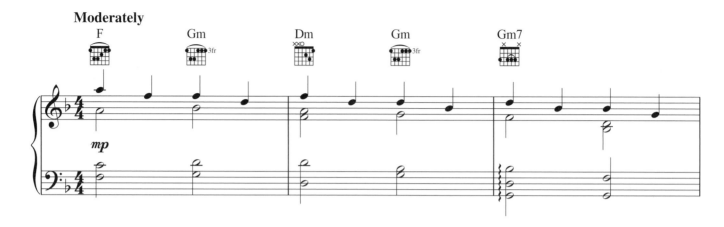

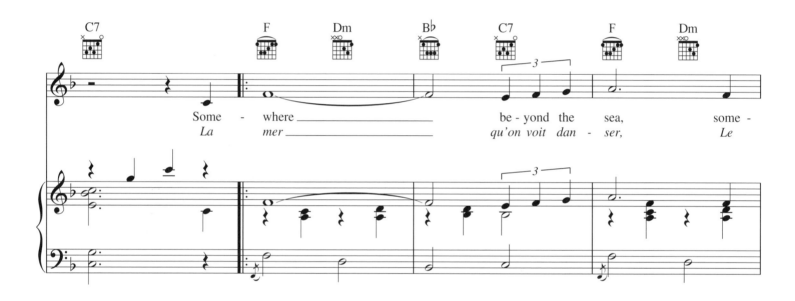

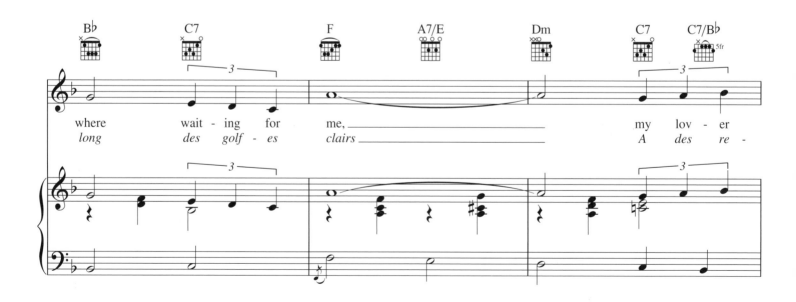

BIG BAD JOHN

Words and Music by
JIMMY DEAN

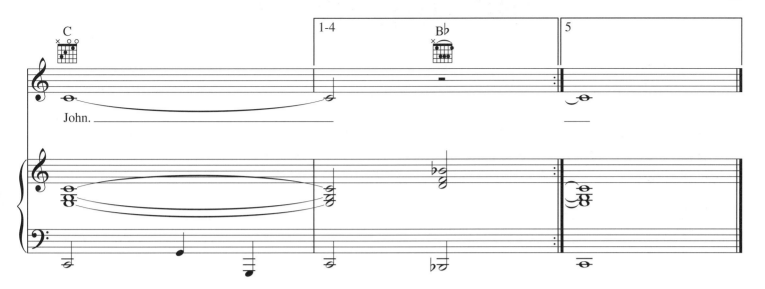

Verses

1. Every morning at the mine you could see him arrive,
   He stood six-foot-six and weighed two-forty-five.
   Kind of broad at the shoulder and narrow at the hip,
   And everybody knew you didn't give no lip to Big John!
   Refrain

2. Nobody seemed to know where John called home,
   He just drifted into town and stayed all alone.
   He didn't say much, a-kinda quiet and shy,
   And if you spoke at all, you just said, "Hi" to Big John!
   Somebody said he came from New Orleans,
   Where he got in a fight over a Cajun queen.
   And a crashing blow from a huge right hand
   Sent a Louisiana fellow to the promised land. Big John!
   Refrain

3. Then came the day at the bottom of the mine
   When a timber cracked and the men started crying.
   Miners were praying and hearts beat fast,
   And everybody thought that they'd breathed their last 'cept John.
   Through the dust and the smoke of this man-made hell
   Walked a giant of a man that the miners knew well.
   Grabbed a sagging timber and gave out with a groan,
   And, like a giant oak tree, just stood there alone. Big John!
   Refrain

4. And with all of his strength, he gave a mighty shove;
   Then a miner yelled out, "There's a light up above!"
   And twenty men scrambled from a would-be grave,
   And now there's only one left down there to save; Big John!
   With jacks and timbers they started back down
   Then came that rumble way down in the ground,
   And smoke and gas belched out of that mine,
   Everybody knew it was the end of the line for Big John!
   Refrain

5. Now they never re-opened that worthless pit,
   They just placed a marble stand in front of it;
   These few words are written on that stand:
   "At the bottom of this mine lies a big, big man; Big John!"
   Refrain

BLOWIN' IN THE WIND

Words and Music by
BOB DYLAN

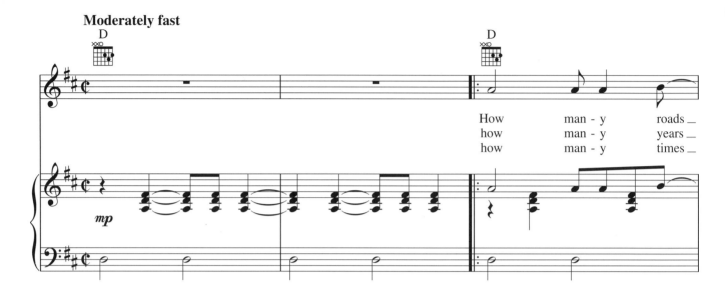

How man-y roads _
how man-y years _
how man-y times _

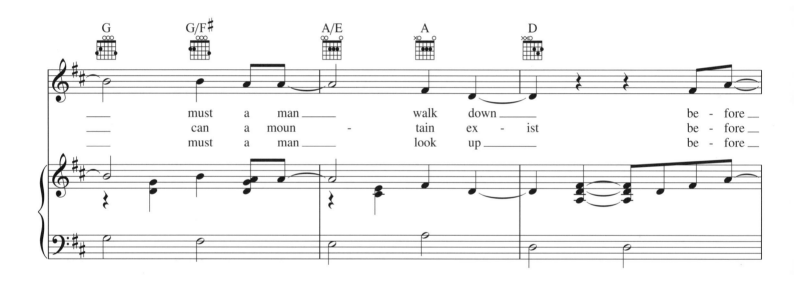

must a man _ walk down _ be - fore _
can a moun - tain ex - ist _ be - fore _
must a man _ look up _ be - fore _

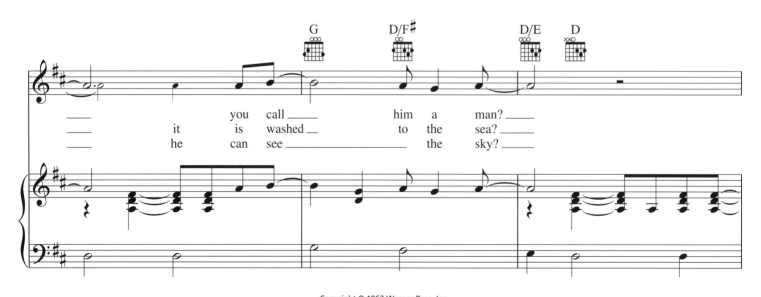

you call _ him a man? _
it is washed _ to the sea? _
he can see _ the sky? _

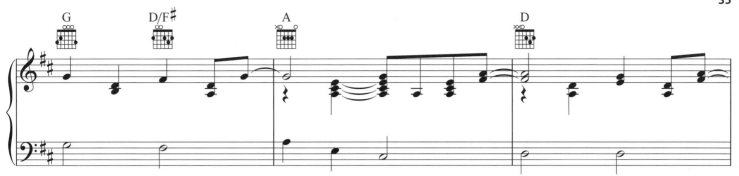

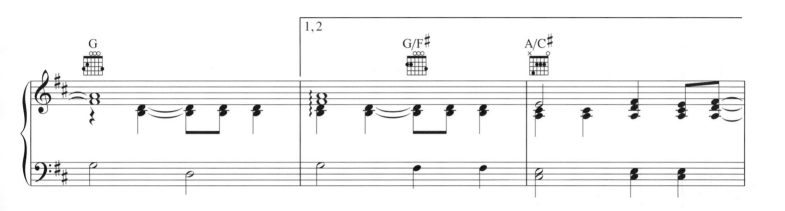

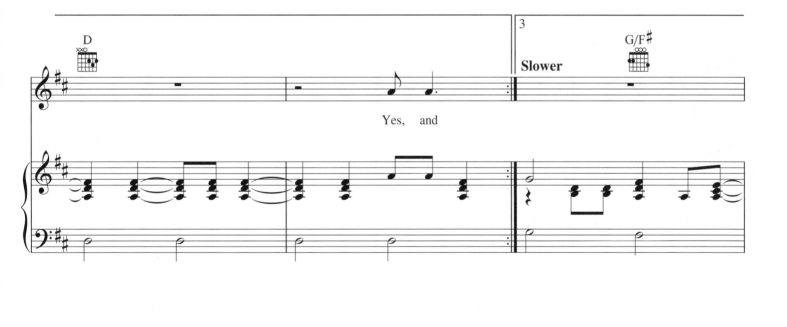

Yes, and

rit.

BLUE VELVET

Words and Music by BERNIE WAYNE
and LEE MORRIS

Slowly, with expression

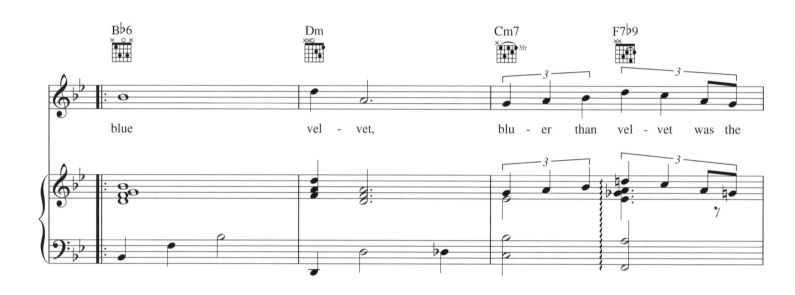

BOBBY'S GIRL

Words and Music by GARY KLEIN
and HENRY HOFFMAN

BREAD AND BUTTER

Words and Music by LARRY PARKS
and JAY TURNBOW

1. I like bread and
2.-4. (See additional lyrics)

but - ter, I like toast and jam.

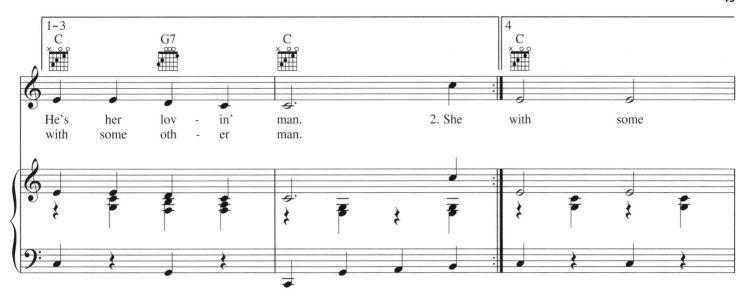

He's her lov - in' man. 2. She with some
with some oth - er man.

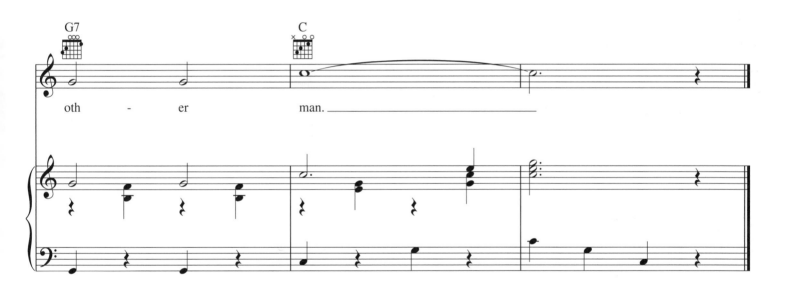

oth - er man. _____

Additional Lyrics

2. She don't cook mashed potatoes,
   Don't cook T-bone steak.
   Don't feed me peanut butter.
   She knows that I can't take.

3. Got home early one mornin'.
   Much to my surprise
   She was eatin' chicken and dumplin's
   With some other guy.

4. No more bread and butter,
   No more toast and jam.
   I found my baby eatin'
   With some other man.

BORN FREE

from the Columbia Pictures' Release BORN FREE

Words by DON BLACK
Music by JOHN BARRY

CALENDAR GIRL

Words and Music by HOWARD GREENFIELD
and NEIL SEDAKA

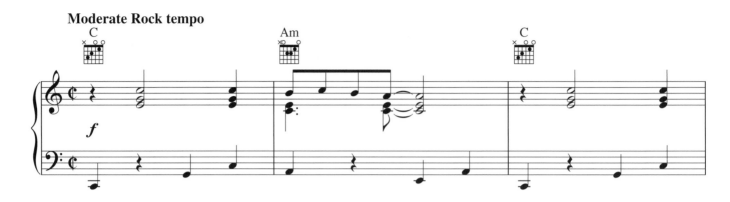

I love, I love, I love my cal-en-dar girl. ___

Yeah, sweet cal-en-dar girl. ___ I love, I love, I love my

CALIFORNIA DREAMIN'

Words and Music by JOHN PHILLIPS
and MICHELLE PHILLIPS

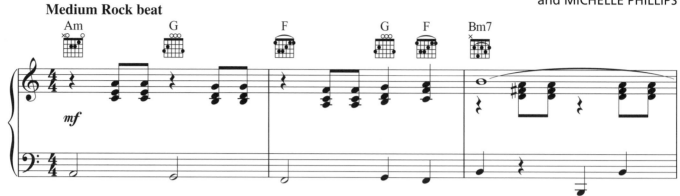

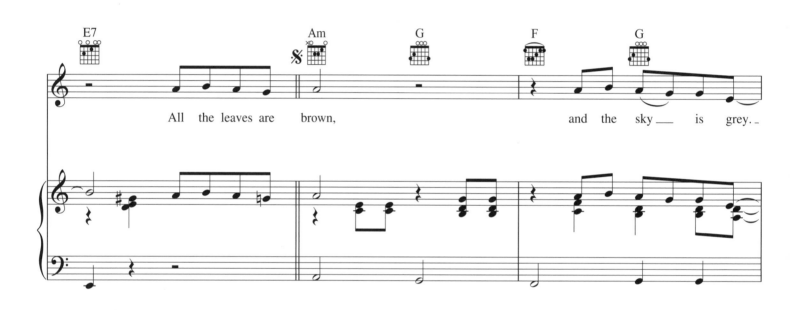

All the leaves are brown, and the sky ___ is grey. ___

I've been ___ for a walk

CARRIE-ANNE

Words and Music by ALLAN CLARKE,
TONY HICKS and GRAHAM NASH

CATHY'S CLOWN

Words and Music by
DON EVERLY

CHERISH

Words and Music by
TERRY KIRKMAN

Moderately

F6/9   Ebmaj7   F6/9   Ebmaj7

mp

F

Gm7/F

Eb

(1.,3.) Cher - ish is the word I use to de - scribe _____
(2.) Per - ish is the word that more than ap - plies _____

C7

F

Gm7/F

all the feel - ing that I have hid - ing here for you in - side. _____
to the hope in my heart each time I re - al - ize _____

Eb

C7

Am

_____ You don't know how man - y times I've wished that I had
_____ that I am not gon - na be the one to share your

CHERRY, CHERRY

Words and Music by
NEIL DIAMOND

Brightly

Ba - by loves _ me, yes, yes, _ she does.
Y'ain't got no _ right, no, no, _ you don't,

Ah, the girl's out - a - sight, _ yeah.
ah, to be so ex - cit - ing.

Says she loves _ me, yes, yes, _ she does.
Won't need bright _ lights, no, no, _ we won't.

To Coda ⊕

Tell your ma - ma, girl, __ I can't stay long.
No, __ we won't __ tell a soul __ where we gone to.

We got things __ we got __ to catch
Girl, we do __ what - ev - er we

up on. Ah, you know, __
want to. Ah, I love __

CRIMSON AND CLOVER

Words and Music by TOMMY JAMES
and PETER LUCIA

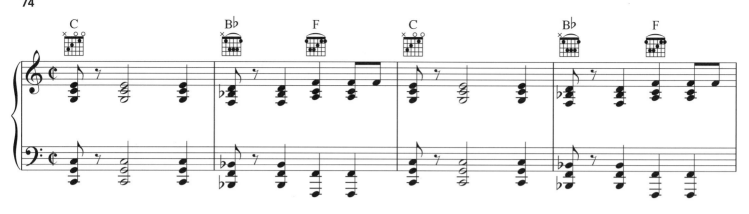

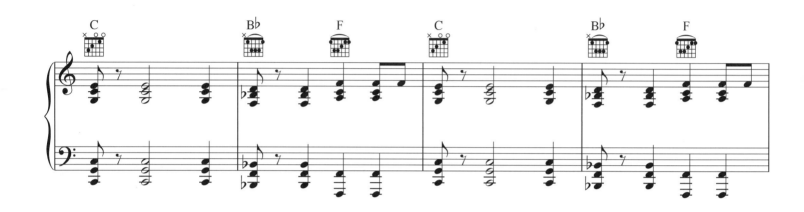

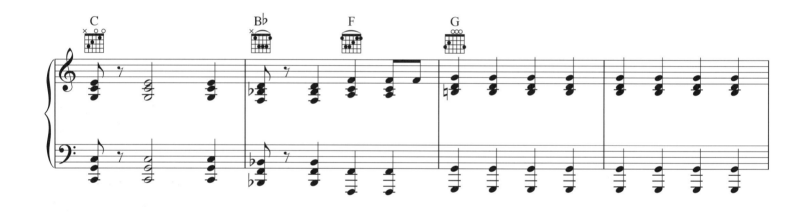

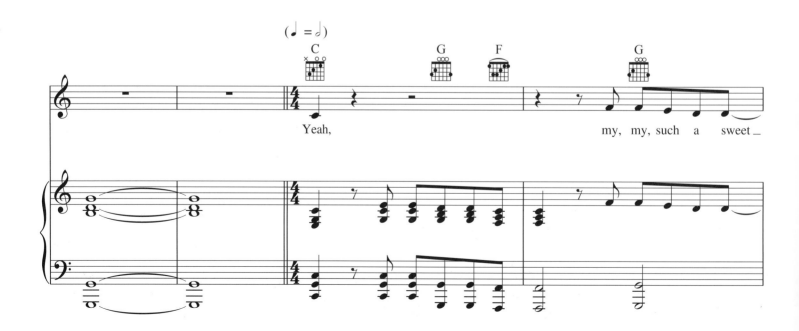

Yeah,

my, my, such a sweet

CRYING

Words and Music by ROY ORBISON
and JOE MELSON

CYCLES

Words and Music by
GAYLE CALDWELL

So I'm down, and so I'm out,
I've been told, and and I be-lieve that
But I'll keep my head up high, al-

life
though
but so are man-y oth-ers.
is meant for liv-in'.
I'm kind-a tired. ____ My

So I feel like try'n' to hide my
E-ven when my chips are low, there's
{gal}
{man}
just up and left last week;

DAYDREAM

Words and Music by
JOHN SEBASTIAN

DO WAH DIDDY DIDDY

Words and Music by JEFF BARRY
and ELLIE GREENWICH

DREAM BABY
(How Long Must I Dream)

Words and Music by
CINDY WALKER

DO YOU BELIEVE IN MAGIC

Words and Music by
JOHN SEBASTIAN

DON'T SLEEP IN THE SUBWAY

Words and Music by TONY HATCH
and JACKIE TRENT

DUKE OF EARL

Words and Music by EARL EDWARDS,
EUGENE DIXON and BERNICE WILLIAMS

EL PASO

Words and Music by
MARTY ROBBINS

Out in the West Tex - as town of El
Night - time would find me in Ro - sa's Can -

Pa - so, I fell in love with a Mex - i - can
ti - na. Mu - sic would play and Fe - li - na would

girl. _____

whirl. _____

Black - er than night were the eyes of Fe - li - na,
Just for a mo - ment, I stood there in si - lence,
Back in El Pa - so my life would be worth - less;
Off to my right I see five mount - ed cow - boys.

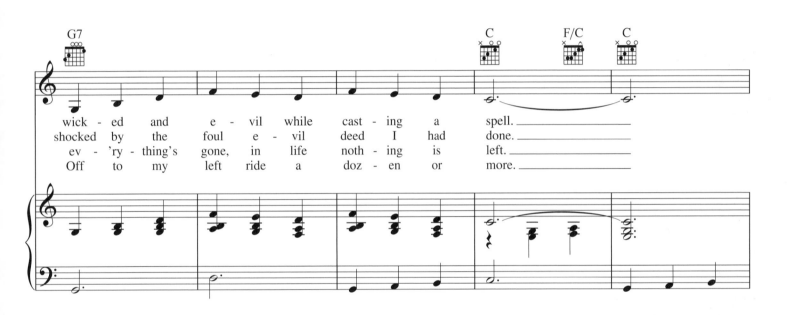

wick - ed and e - vil while cast - ing a spell. _____
shocked by the foul e - vil deed I had done. _____
ev - 'ry - thing's gone, in life noth - ing is left. _____
Off to my left ride a doz - en or more. _____

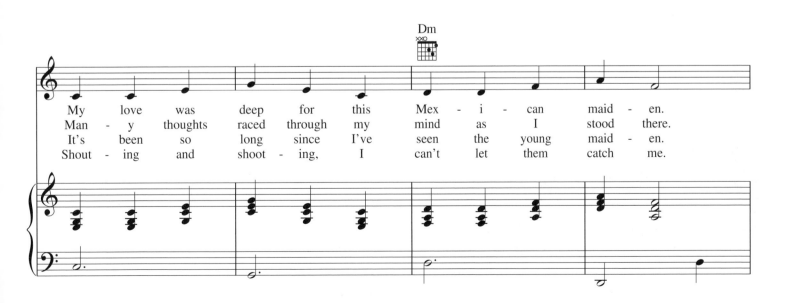

My love was deep for this Mex - i - can maid - en.
Man - y thoughts raced through my mind as I stood there.
It's been so long since I've seen the young maid - en.
Shout - ing and shoot - ing, I can't let them catch me.

I was in love, but in vain, I could tell. _____
I had but one chance, and that was to run. _____
My love is strong - er than my fear of death. _____
I have to make it to Ro - sa's back door. _____

One night a wild young cow - boy came in,
Out through the wild back door of Ro - sa's I ran
I sad - dled up and a - way I did go,
Some - thing is dread - ful - ly wrong for I feel a

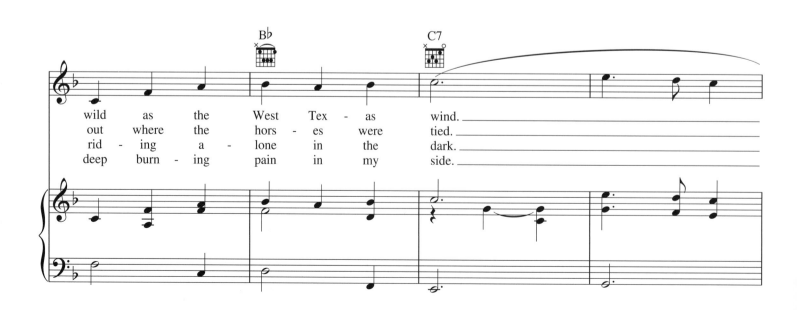

wild as the West Tex - as wind. _____
out where the hors - es were tied. _____
rid - ing a - lone in the dark. _____
deep burn - ing pain in my side. _____

Dash - ing and dar - ing, a
I caught a good one, it
May - be to - mor - row a
Though I am try - ing to

drink he was shar - ing with wick - ed Fe - li - na, the
looked like it could run. Up on its back and a -
bul - let will find me. To - night, noth - ing's worse than this
stay in the sad - dle, I'm get - ting wea - ry, un -

girl that I loved. So, in an - ger, I
way I did ride just as fast as I
pain in my heart. And at last, here I
a - ble to ride. But my love for Fe -

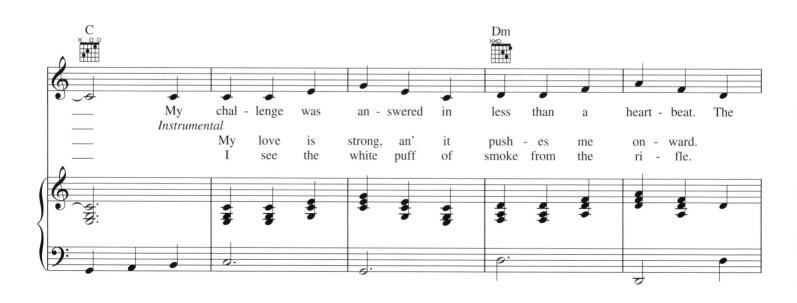

Play 4 times

hand - some young stran - ger lay dead on the floor. _____
Down off the hill to Fe - li - na I go. _____
I feel the bul - let go deep in my chest. _____

Instrumental ends

From out of no - where, Fe - li - na has found me,
Cra - dled by two lov - ing arms that I'll die for,

kiss - ing my cheek as she kneels by my side. _____
one lit - tle kiss, then Fe - li - na, good -

bye. _____

ELEANOR RIGBY

Words and Music by JOHN LENNON
and PAUL McCARTNEY

Moderately, with a steady beat

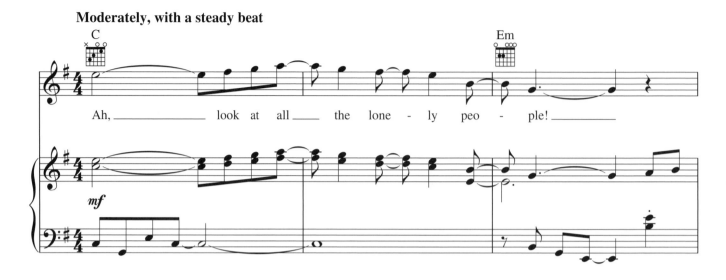

Ah, _____ look at all _____ the lone - ly peo - ple! _____

Ah, _____ look at all _____ the lone - ly peo -

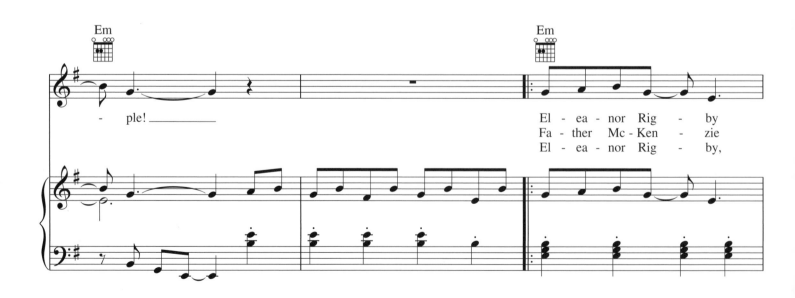

-ple! _____

El - ea - nor Rig - by
Fa - ther Mc - Ken - zie
El - ea - nor Rig - by,

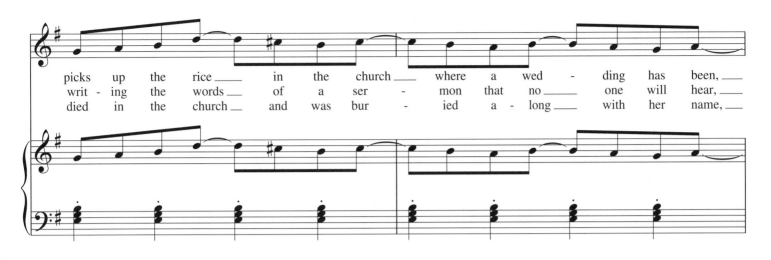

picks up the rice ___ in the church ___ where a wed - ding has been, ___
writ - ing the words ___ of a ser - mon that no ___ one will hear, ___
died in the church ___ and was bur - ied a - long ___ with her name, ___

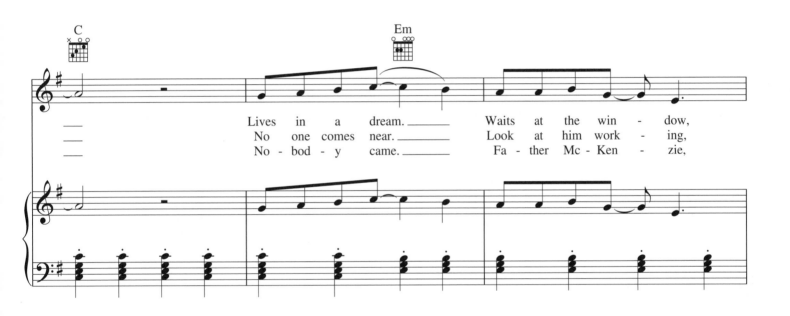

C   Em

___ Lives in a dream. ___ Waits at the win - dow,
___ No one comes near. ___ Look at him work - ing,
___ No - bod - y came. ___ Fa - ther Mc - Ken - zie,

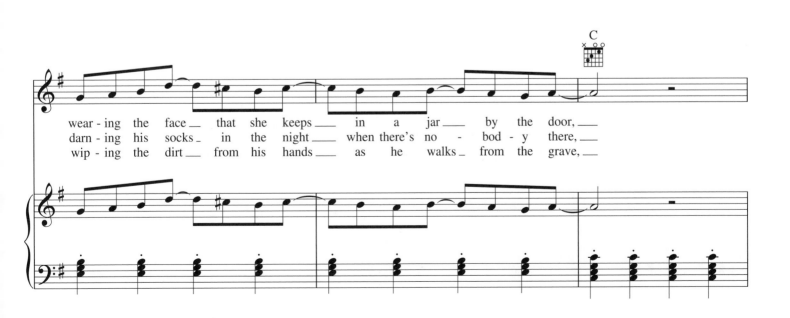

C

wear - ing the face ___ that she keeps ___ in a jar ___ by the door, ___
darn - ing his socks ___ in the night ___ when there's no - bod - y there, ___
wip - ing the dirt ___ from his hands ___ as he walks ___ from the grave, ___

FERRY 'CROSS THE MERSEY

Words and Music by
GERRARD MARSDEN

FUN, FUN, FUN

Words and Music by BRIAN WILSON
and MIKE LOVE

Bright Rock-Boogie beat

Well, she got her dad - dy's car and she cruised through the ham - burg - er stand ___
girls can't stand her 'cause she walks, looks and drives like an ace ___

___ now. ___
___ now. ___

Seems she for - got all a - bout ___ the li -
She makes the In - dy Five Hun - dred look

brar - y like she told her old man ___ now. ___
like a Ro - man char - i - ot race ___ now. ___

And with her
A lot - ta

GAMES PEOPLE PLAY

Words and Music by
JOE SOUTH

GO AWAY, LITTLE GIRL

Words and Music by GERRY GOFFIN
and CAROLE KING

Moderately slow

Go a-way, ___ lit-tle girl, ___ go a-way, ___ lit-tle girl. ___ I'm not sup-posed to be a-lone with you. ___ I know that your lips are

GROOVIN'

Words and Music by FELIX CAVALIERE
and EDWARD BRIGATI, JR.

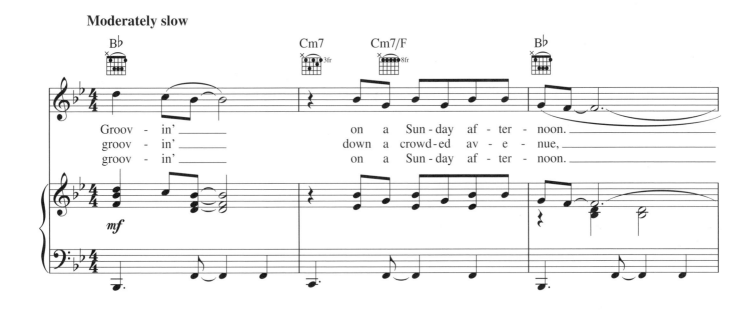

Groov - in' _____ on a Sun - day af - ter - noon. _____
groov - in' _____ down a crowd - ed av - e - nue, _____
groov - in' _____ on a Sun - day af - ter - noon. _____

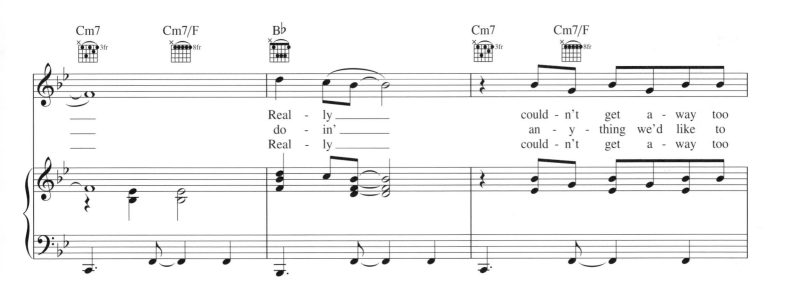

Real - ly _____ could - n't get a - way too
do - in' _____ an - y - thing we'd like to
Real - ly _____ could - n't get a - way too

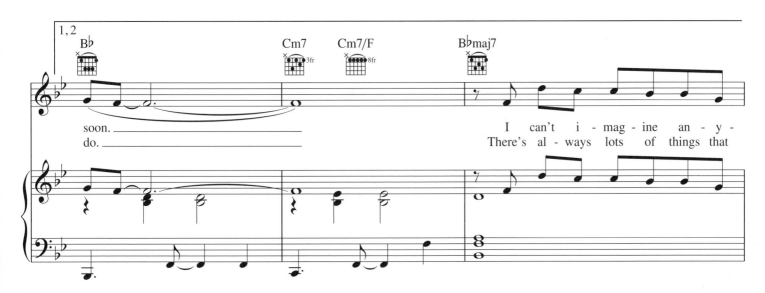

soon. _____
do. _____

I can't i - mag - ine an - y -
There's al - ways lots of things that

Repeat and Fade

GOODBYE CRUEL WORLD

Words and Music by
GLORIA SHAYNE

Moderate Rock

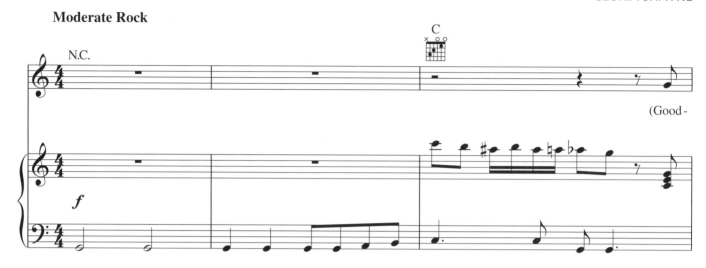

(Good-

bye,   cruel world.)   (Good - bye, cruel world.)   Oh, good-

bye   cruel _ world.   I'm   off   to join the cir - cus.   I'm gon - na be   a
well   to ___ love.   I'm   off   to join the cir - cus.   Got - ta find   a

GREENFIELDS

Words and Music by TERRY GILKYSON,
RICHARD DEHR and FRANK MILLER

HAPPY TOGETHER

Words and Music by GARRY BONNER
and ALAN GORDON

HARPER VALLEY P.T.A.

Words and Music by
TOM T. HALL

I want to tell you all a story 'bout a Har-per Val-ley wid-owed wife _____ who had a teen-age daugh-ter who at-tend-ed Har-per Val-ley Ju-nior

note said, "Mis-sus John-son, you're wear-ing your dress-es way too high. It's re- port-ed you've been drink-ing and a run-nin' 'round with men and go-ing

hap-pened that the P. T. A. was gon-na meet that ver-y af-ter-noon. They were sure sur-prised when Mis-sus John-son wore her min-i-skirt in-to the

HAWAII FIVE-O THEME
from the Television Series

By MORT STEVENS

HE'LL HAVE TO GO

Words and Music by JOE ALLISON
and AUDREY ALLISON

Moderately

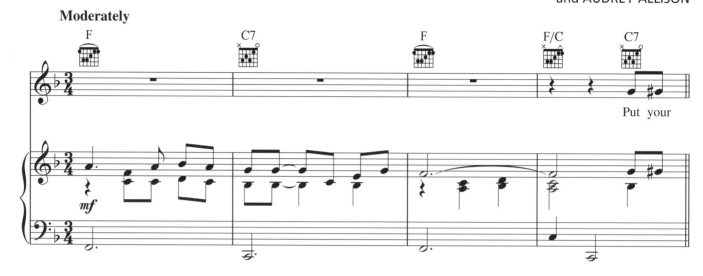

Put your

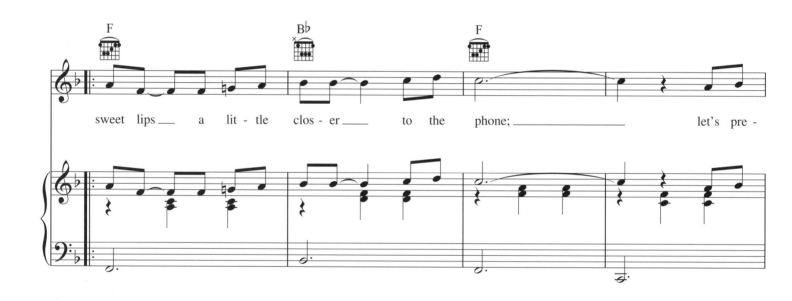

sweet lips — a lit-tle clos-er — to the phone; _____ let's pre-

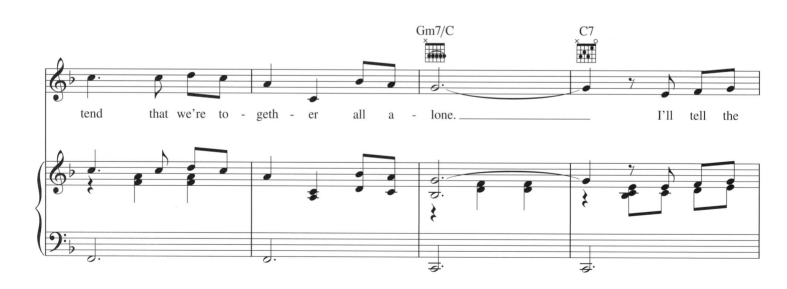

tend that we're to-geth-er all a-lone. _____ I'll tell the

HELLO MARY LOU

Words and Music by GENE PITNEY
and C. MANGIARACINA

passed me by one sun-ny day,_____ flashed those big brown
saw your lips, I heard your voice.____ Be - lieve me, I just

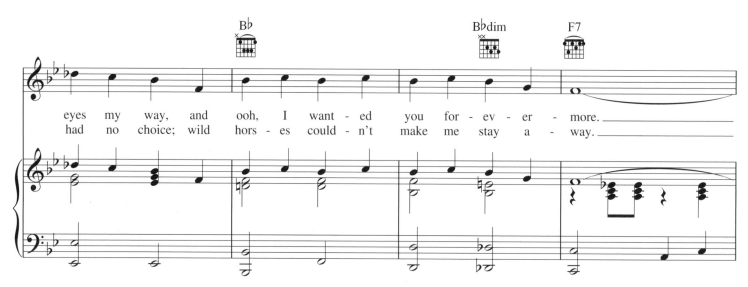

eyes my way, and ooh, I want - ed you for - ev - er - more._____
had no choice; wild hors - es could - n't make me stay a - way._____

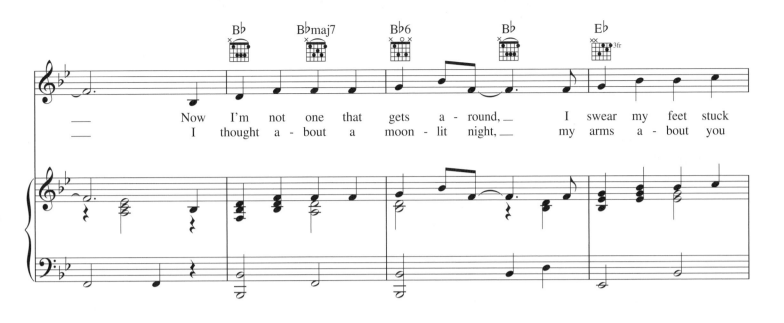

Now I'm not one that gets a - round, __ I swear my feet stuck
I thought a - bout a moon - lit night, __ my arms a - bout you

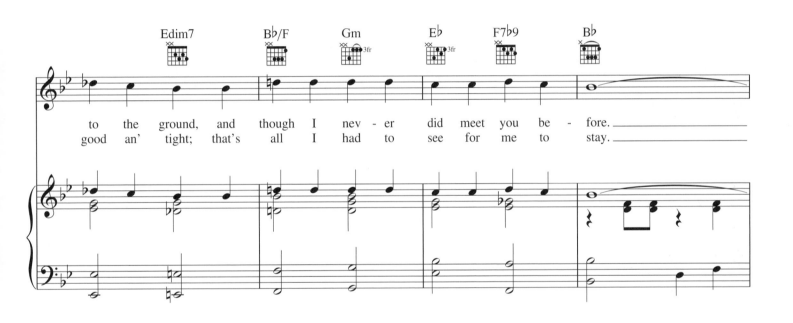

to the ground, and though I nev - er did meet you be - fore. _____
good an' tight; that's all I had to see for me to stay. _____

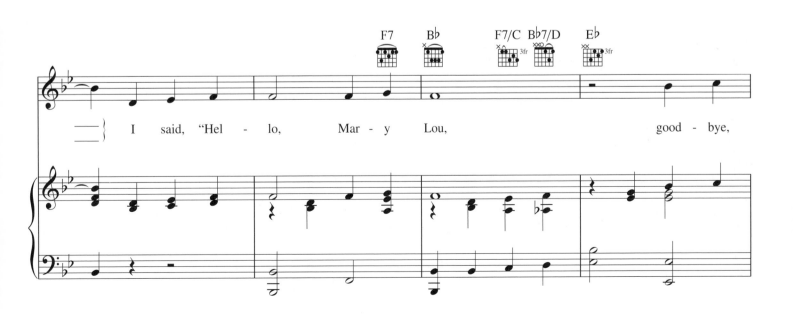

__ I said, "Hel - lo, Mar - y Lou, good - bye,

heart. Sweet Mar - y Lou, I'm so in love with you. _____

Knew, Mar - y Lou, we'd nev - er part, so hel - lo, Mar - y

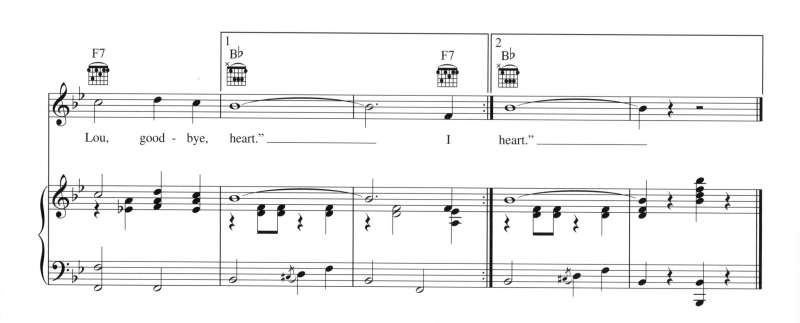

Lou, good - bye, heart." _____ I heart." _____

HOOKED ON A FEELING

Words and Music by
MARK JAMES

I CAN'T HELP MYSELF
(Sugar Pie, Honey Bunch)

Words and Music by BRIAN HOLLAND,
LAMONT DOZIER and EDWARD HOLLAND

Sug - ar pie, hon - ey bunch, you know that I
Sug - ar pie, hon - ey bunch, I'm weak - er than a

love you. I can't help my - self,
man should be. I can't help my - self,

I GET AROUND

Words and Music by BRIAN WILSON
and MIKE LOVE

Medium bright Rock beat

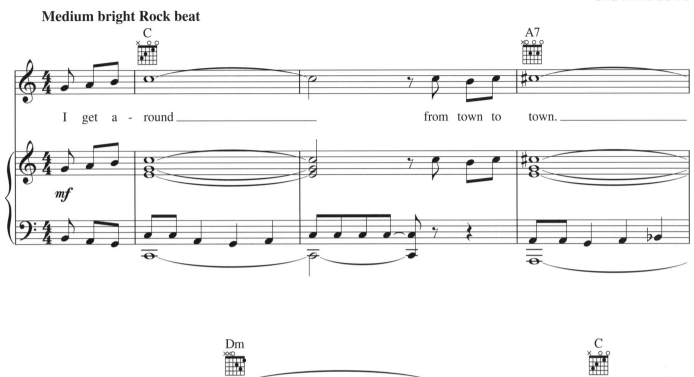

I get a-round _____ from town to town. _____

_____ I'm a real cool head, _____ I'm mak-in' real good bread. __

I'm get-tin' bugged driv-in' up an' down the
al - ways take my car 'cause it's

I HEAR A SYMPHONY

Words and Music by EDWARD HOLLAND,
LAMONT DOZIER and BRIAN HOLLAND

You've giv-en me a true love, and ev-'ry day I thank _ you, love,

for a feel-ing that's _ so new, _ so in-vit-ing, so ex-cit-ing.

When-ev-er you are near, I hear a sym-pho-ny, a ten-der

I KNOW A PLACE

Words and Music by
TONY HATCH

I LEFT MY HEART IN SAN FRANCISCO

Words by DOUGLASS CROSS
Music by GEORGE CORY

Am7　　　D7♭9　　　Gm7　　　　　　　　C9　　　C7♭9

The morn - ing fog _____ may chill the

F9sus　　　F9　Bdim7　Cm7　　　F7　C#dim7　B♭maj9

air;　　　　I don't care! My love waits there

C#dim7　　Cm7

in San Fran - cis - co, _____ a - bove the

F9　　　E♭6/G　　　F7/A　E♭/G　E♭6　　D　　　C/E

blue _____ and wind - y sea.

I SAY A LITTLE PRAYER

Lyric by HAL DAVID
Music by BURT BACHARACH

Moderately fast

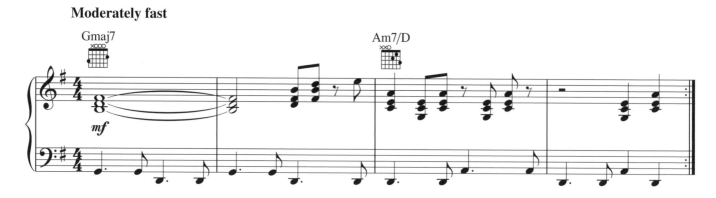

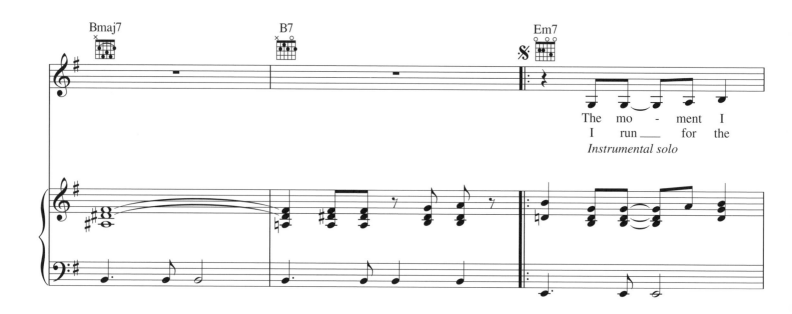

The mo - ment I
I run ___ for the
Instrumental solo

wake up,
be - fore ___ I put on my make - up, I
bus, dear.
While rid - ing, I think of us, dear. I
(I

IF I WERE A CARPENTER

Words and Music by
TIM HARDIN

If I ____ were a car- pen- ter, ____
If I ____ worked my hands in wood, __

and you were a la- dy,
would you still ____ love me?

would you mar- ry me
An- swer me, ___ babe,

I WILL FOLLOW HIM
(I Will Follow You)

English Words by NORMAN GIMBEL and ARTHUR ALTMAN
French Words by JACQUES PLANTE
Music by J.W. STOLE and DEL ROMA

I'M A BELIEVER

Words and Music by
NEIL DIAMOND

I'M SORRY

Words and Music by RONNIE SELF
and DUB ALBRITTEN

IN THE MIDNIGHT HOUR

Words and Music by STEVE CROPPER
and WILSON PICKETT

LAST TRAIN TO CLARKSVILLE

Words and Music by BOBBY HART
and TOMMY BOYCE

Take the last train to Clarks-ville and I'll
last train to Clarks-ville, I'll be

meet you at the sta-tion. You can be there by four
wait-ing at the sta-tion. We'll have time for cof-fee

thir-ty 'cause I've made your res-er-va-tion. Don't be
fla-vored kiss-es and a bit of con-ver-sa-tion.

IT'S MY PARTY

Words and Music by HERB WIENER,
WALLY GOLD and JOHN GLUCK, JR.

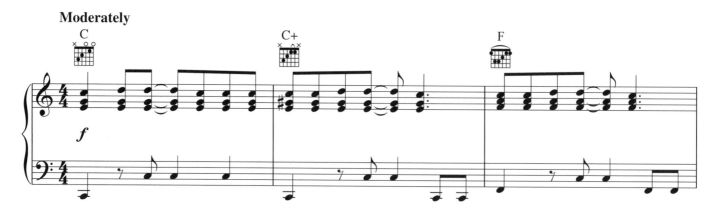

No-bod-y knows _ where my John-ny has gone, _ but
Play all my rec - ords, keep danc-ing all night, _ but
Ju-dy and John - ny just walked through the door, _

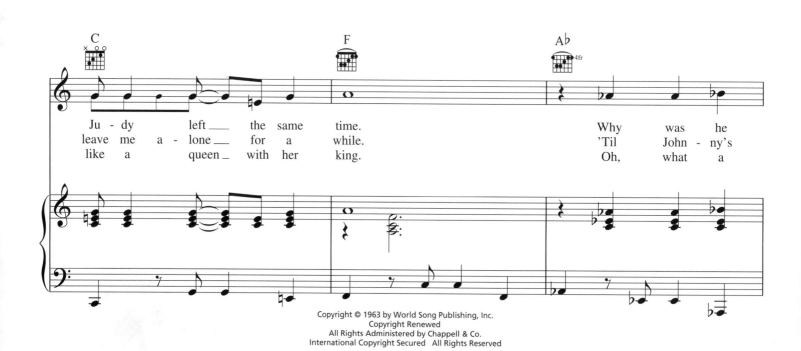

Ju-dy left _ the same time.
leave me a - lone _ for a while.
like a queen _ with her king.

Why was he
'Til John-ny's
Oh, what a

hold-ing her hand, — when he's sup-posed — to be mine? ___
danc-ing with me, — I've got no rea-son to smile. ___
birth-day sur-prise; — Ju-dy's wear-ing his ring. ___

It's my par-ty, and I'll cry if I want — to, cry if I want — to,

cry if I want — to. You would cry, too, if it hap-pened to

you.

KING OF THE ROAD

Words and Music by
ROGER MILLER

man of means ___ by no means, king of the road. ___

I know ev-er-y en-gi-neer on ev-er-y train, ___ all of the chil - dren and

all of their names, ___ and ev-er-y hand-out in ev-er-y town, ___ and

ev-'ry lock that ain't locked when no one's a - round. ___ I sing:

LEADER OF THE PACK

Words and Music by GEORGE MORTON,
JEFF BARRY and ELLIE GREENWICH

Ad Lib.

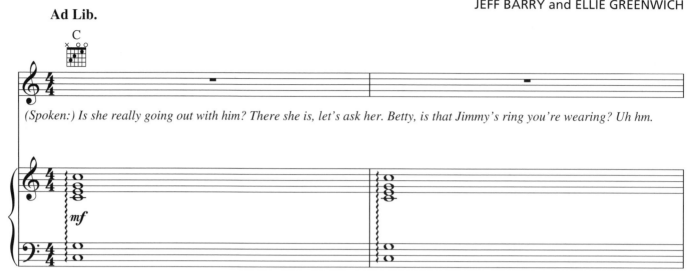

(Spoken:) Is she really going out with him? There she is, let's ask her. Betty, is that Jimmy's ring you're wearing? Uh hm.

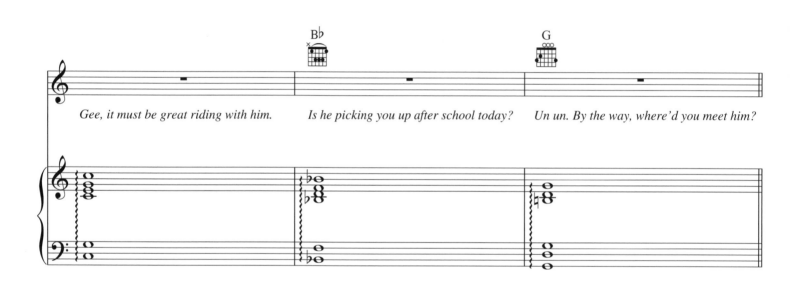

Gee, it must be great riding with him.   Is he picking you up after school today?   Un un. By the way, where'd you meet him?

Moderately, with a beat

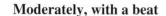

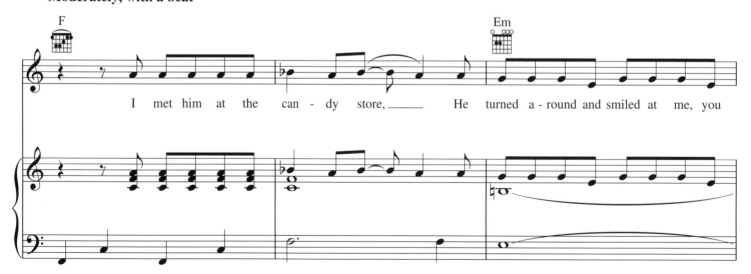

I met him at the can-dy store,___ He turned a-round and smiled at me, you

LEAVING ON A JET PLANE

Words and Music by
JOHN DENVER

213

LIMBO ROCK

Words and Music by BILLY STRANGE
and JON SHELDON

Moderately slow Calypso

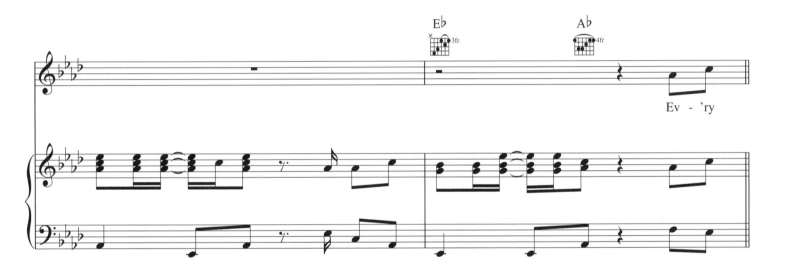

Ev - 'ry

lim - bo boy ___ and girl all a - round the lim - bo world gon - na

spread your lim - bo feet, then you move to lim - bo beat. Lim - bo

self a lim - bo girl, give that chick a lim - bo whirl. There's a

LIGHTNIN' STRIKES

Words and Music by LOU CHRISTIE
and TWYLA HERBERT

LITTLE GREEN APPLES

Words and Music by
BOBBY RUSSELL

When I wake up in the morn-ing with my hair down in my eyes and she says, "Hi," ___

And I stum-ble to the break-fast ta-ble while the kids are go-ing off to school, good

bye. ___

And she reach-es out an' takes my hand,

THE LITTLE OLD LADY
(From Pasadena)

Words and Music by DON ALTFELD
and ROGER CHRISTIAN

The lit-tle old la-dy from Pas-a-de-na
see her on the strip don't try to choose ___ her.
see her all the time, just get-tin' her kicks ___ now,

(Go Gran-ny, go Gran-ny, go Gran-ny, go.) ___
has a pret-ty lit-tle flow-er bed of
You might have ___ a ___ go-er, but you'll
with her four-speed ___ stick ___ and a

LOUIE, LOUIE

Words and Music by
RICHARD BERRY

* Lyrics omitted at the request of the publisher.

A LOVER'S CONCERTO

Words and Music by SANDY LINZER
and DENNY RANDELL

How gen-tle is the rain that falls soft-ly on the mead-ow.

MELLOW YELLOW

Words and Music by
DONOVAN LEITCH

1. I'm just mad a-bout Saf - fron. _____ Saf - fron's mad a-bout me. _____
2. I'm just mad a-bout Four - teen. _____ Four - teen's mad a-bout me. _____
3. Born high, for-ev - er to fly. _____ Wind ve - loc - i - ty, nil. _____
4. - 6. (See additional lyrics)

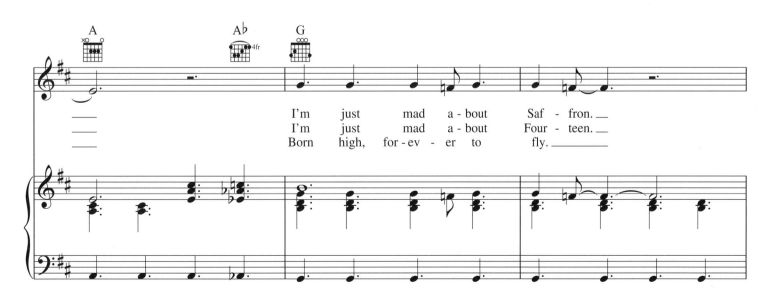

I'm just mad a - bout Saf - fron. _____
I'm just mad a - bout Four - teen. _____
Born high, for - ev - er to fly. _____

She's just mad a - bout me. ——
She's just mad a - bout me. ——
If you want your cup, I will fill. ——

They call me Mel - low Yel - low, —

Chorus

they call me Mel - low Yel - low, ——

they call me Mel - low

Yel - low. ——

1 - 4

Yel - low. ___

They call me Mel - low

Yel - low. ___

They call me Mel - low

Yel - low. ___

Optional Ending

Repeat and Fade

Additional Lyrics

4. *Instrumental*
   Chorus

5. Electrical banana
   Is going to be a sudden craze.
   Electrical banana
   Is bound to be the very next phase.
   Chorus

6. I'm just mad about Saffron.
   I'm just mad about her.
   I'm just mad about Saffron.
   She's just mad about me.
   Chorus

MAGIC CARPET RIDE

Words and Music by JOHN KAY
and RUSHTON MOREVE

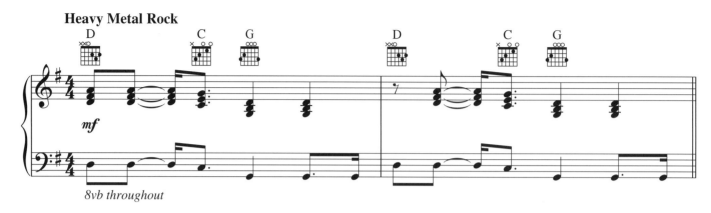

I like ____ to dream _____

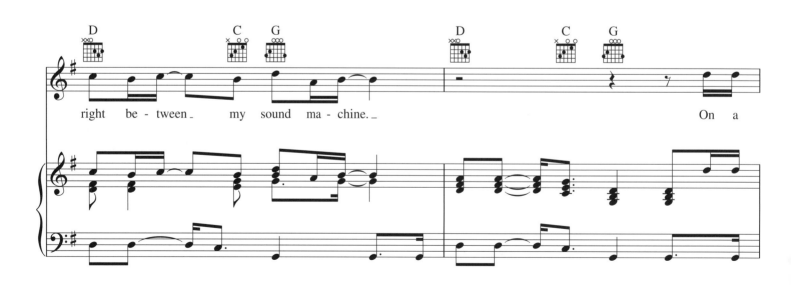

right be-tween ___ my sound ma-chine. ___ On a

MONDAY, MONDAY

Words and Music by
JOHN PHILLIPS

MY GIRL

Words and Music by WILLIAM "SMOKEY" ROBINSON
and RONALD WHITE

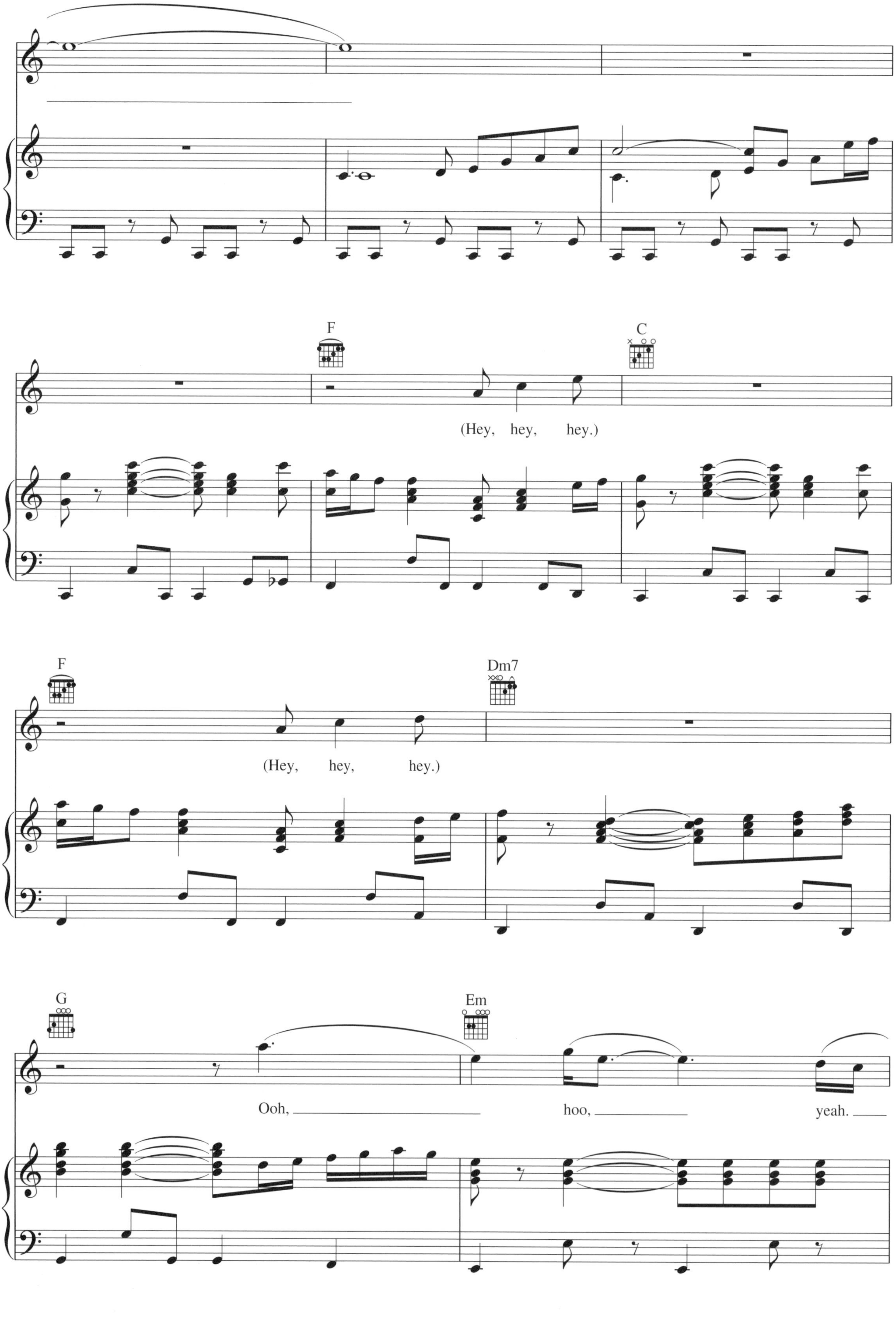
F
C
(Hey, hey, hey.)
F
Dm7
(Hey, hey, hey.)
G
Em
Ooh,
hoo,
yeah.

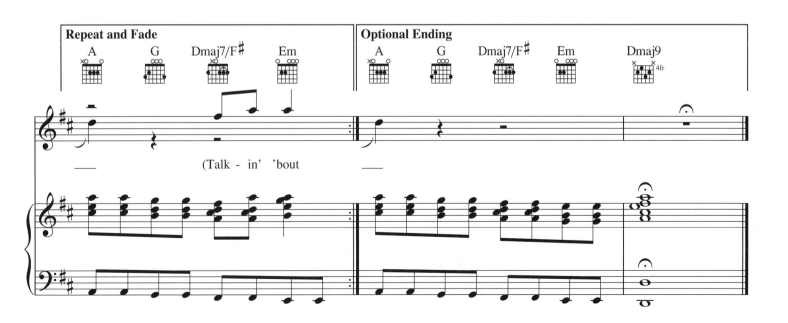

MY BOYFRIEND'S BACK

Words and Music by ROBERT FELDMAN,
GERALD GOLDSTEIN and RICHARD GOTTEHRER

Repeat and Fade

Na Na Hey Hey Kiss Him Goodbye

Words and Music by ARTHUR FRASHUER DALE,
PAUL ROGER LEKA and GARY CARLA

(You Make Me Feel Like)
A NATURAL WOMAN

Words and Music by GERRY GOFFIN,
CAROLE KING and JERRY WEXLER

OH, PRETTY WOMAN

Words and Music by ROY ORBISON
and BILL DEES

Hey, O. K.

If that's the way it must be ___ O. K.

I guess I'll go on home, ___ it's late ___ There'll be to-

mor - row night but wait! What do I see? ___

ON BROADWAY

Words and Music by BARRY MANN, CYNTHIA WEIL,
MIKE STOLLER and JERRY LEIBER

Moderately, with a beat

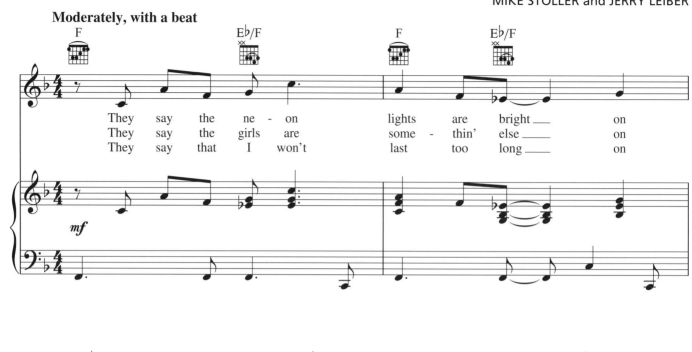

They say the ne - on lights are bright ___ on
They say the girls are some - thin' else ___ on
They say that I won't last too long ___ on

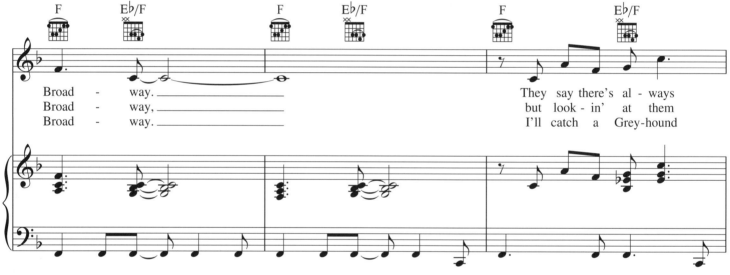

Broad - way. _____
Broad - way, _____
Broad - way. _____

They say there's al - ways
but look - in' at them
I'll catch a Grey-hound

mag - ic in ___ the air. _____
just gives me ___ the blues, _____
bus for home, ___ they all say. _____

ONE FINE DAY

Words and Music by GERRY GOFFIN
and CAROLE KING

One _____ fine day _____
The arms I long for _____
One _____ fine day _____

you'll look at me, _____
will o - pen wide, _____
we'll meet once more, _____

and you will know _____ our love was meant _____ to
and you'll be proud _____ to have me walk - ing by
and then you'll want _____ the love you threw a - way

PEPPERMINT TWIST

Words and Music by JOSEPH DiNICOLA
and HENRY GLOVER

PROUD MARY

Words and Music by
JOHN FOGERTY

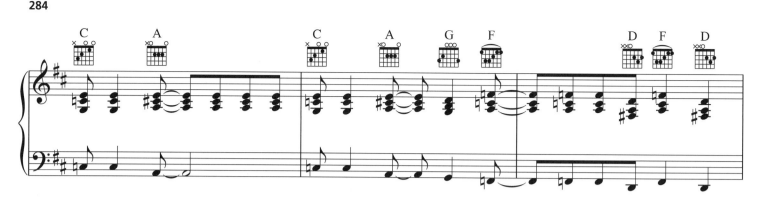

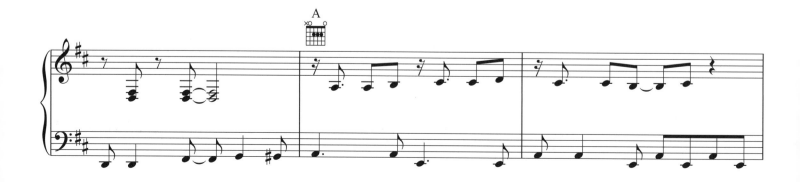

Roll - in', roll -
- in', roll - in' on the riv - er.

D.S. al Coda

RETURN TO SENDER

Words and Music by OTIS BLACKWELL
and WINFIELD SCOTT

PUPPY LOVE

Words and Music by
PAUL ANKA

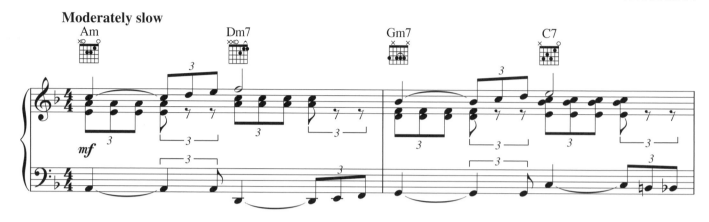

And they called it pup - py

love, _____ oh, I guess they'll nev - er know,

RELEASE ME

Words and Music by ROBERT YOUNT,
EDDIE MILLER and DUB WILLIAMS

Moderately slow

Please **re** - lease me, let me go,

I have found a new love, dear, _____

Please **re** - lease me, can't you see _____

— for I don't love you an - y -

— and I will al - ways want her

— you'd be a fool to cling to

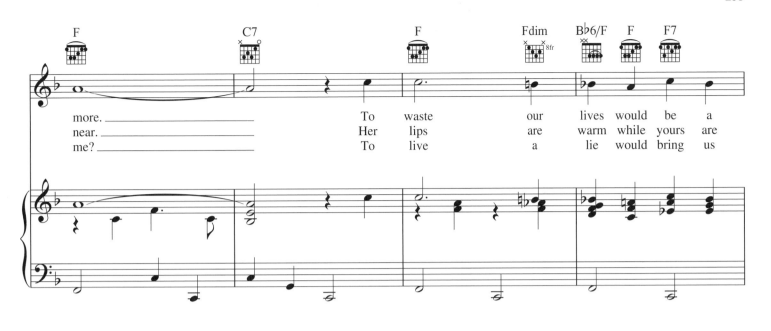

more. _____
near. _____
me? _____

To waste our lives would be a
Her lips are warm while yours are
To live a lie would bring us

sin; _____
cold; _____
pain, _____

re - lease me and let me love a -
re - lease me, my dar - ling, let me
so re - lease me and let me love a -

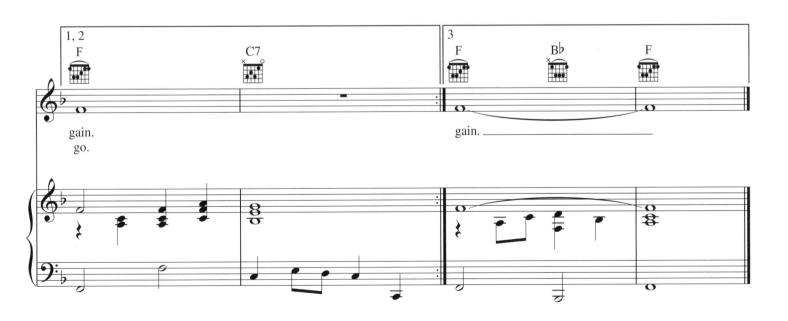

1, 2

gain.
go.

3

gain. _____

RUNAWAY

Words and Music by DEL SHANNON
and MAX CROOK

Moderately

As I walk a-long, __ I won-der

what went wrong __ with our love, a love that was __ so

Tears are fall-in' and I feel a pain, _____ a - wish-in' you were here by me _____ to end this mis - er - y. _____ And I won - der, wo - wo - wo - wo - won - der _____ why, _____ why why why why

SAN FRANCISCO
(Be Sure to Wear Some Flowers in Your Hair)

Words and Music by
JOHN PHILLIPS

SEALED WITH A KISS

Words by PETER UDELL
Music by GARY GELD

SOMEBODY TO LOVE

Words and Music by
DARBY SLICK

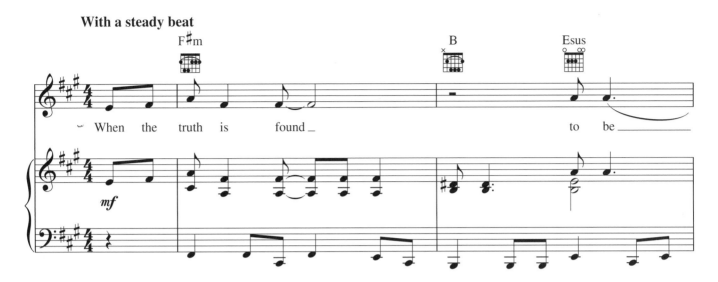

When the truth is found __ to be __

lies, and all __ the joy __

with - in you __ dies, don't you __

(Sittin' On)
THE DOCK OF THE BAY

Words and Music by STEVE CROPPER
and OTIS REDDING

noth-in's gon-na change; __ ev-'ry-thing still __ re-mains the same. __

I can't do what ten peo-ple tell me __ to do, __ so I guess I'll re-main __

the same. __

CODA

D.S. al Coda

Repeat and Fade

Optional Ending

SOUL MAN

Words and Music by ISAAC HAYES
and DAVID PORTER

SPANISH EYES

Words by CHARLES SINGLETON and EDDIE SNYDER
Music by BERT KAEMPFERT

STRANGERS IN THE NIGHT
adapted from A MAN COULD GET KILLED

Words by CHARLES SINGLETON and EDDIE SNYDER
Music by BERT KAEMPFERT

SPANISH FLEA

Words and Music by
JULIUS WECHTER

There was a lit- tle Span- ish flea. ___ A rec- ord star he thought he'd be. ___ He'd heard of sing- ers like Bea- tles, The Chip- munks he'd seen ___ on T- V. _____ Why not a lit- tle Span- ish

SPINNING WHEEL

Words and Music by
DAVID CLAYTON THOMAS

Moderately slow, with a beat

What goes up must come down,

spin - ning wheel got to go 'round. Talk - in' 'bout your trou - bles, it's a

cry - in' sin, ride a paint - ed po - ny, let the spin - ning wheel spin.

Repeat and Fade

SUGAR, SUGAR

Words and Music by ANDY KIM
and JEFF BARRY

SUKIYAKI

Words and Music by HACHIDAI NAKAMURA
and ROKUSUKE EI
English Lyrics by TOM LESLIE
and BUZZ CASON

TAKE GOOD CARE OF MY BABY

Words and Music by GERRY GOFFIN
and CAROLE KING

My tears are fall - in' 'cause you're tak - in' her a - way, _____ and

though it real - ly hurts me so, there's some-thin' that I got - ta say.

Moderately, with a beat

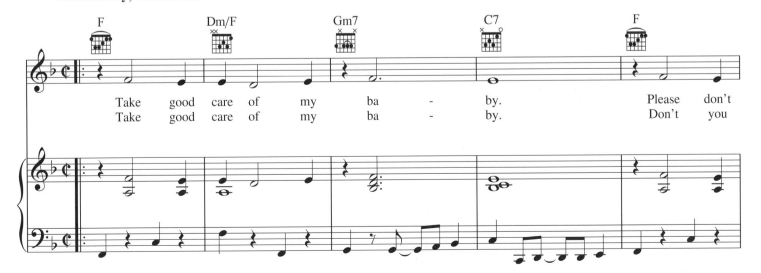

Take good care of my ba - by. Please don't
Take good care of my ba - by. Don't you

TEEN ANGEL

Words and Music by
JEAN SURREY

THESE BOOTS ARE MADE FOR WALKIN'

Words and Music by
LEE HAZLEWOOD

You keep say - in' you got some - thin'
You keep ly - in' when you ought - a be
You keep play - in' where you should - n't be

for me, some - thin' you call
"truth - in'," you keep los - in'
play - in', you keep think - in'

love but con - fess.
when you ought - a not bet.
that you'll nev - er get burned.

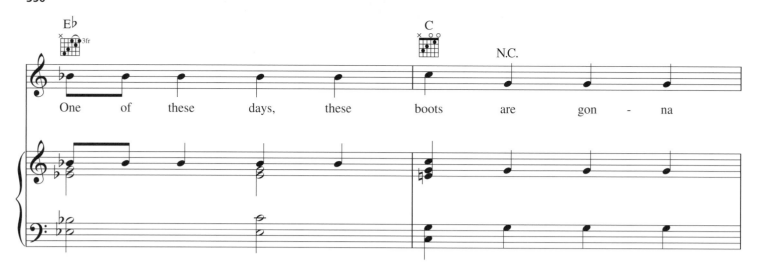

One of these days, these boots are gon - na

walk all o - ver you. _____

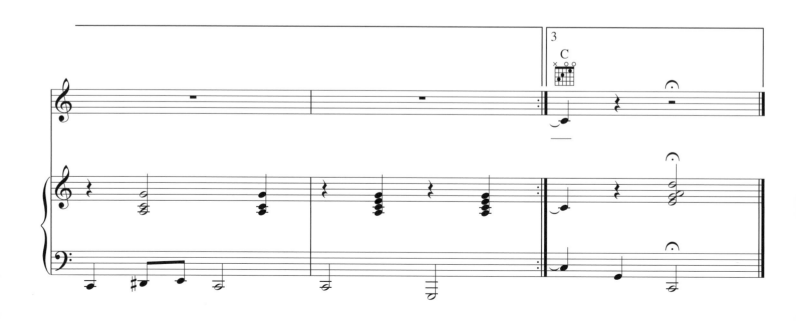

THOSE WERE THE DAYS

Words and Music by
GENE RASKIN

TO SIR, WITH LOVE

Words by DON BLACK
Music by MARC LONDON

Those school girl days
The time has come
Those awk - ward years

of tell - ing
for clos - ing
have hur - ried

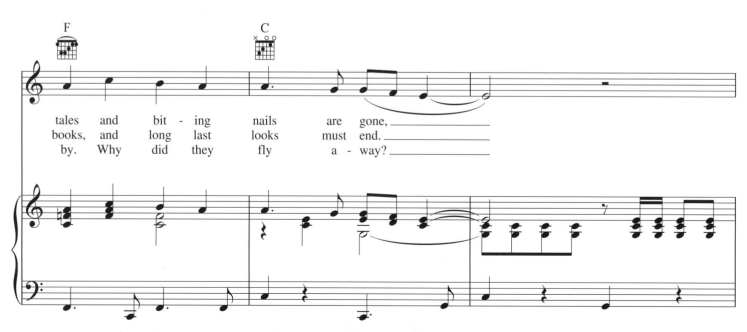

tales and bit - ing nails are gone, _____
books, and long last looks must end. _____
by. Why did they fly a - way? _____

WHAT THE WORLD NEEDS NOW IS LOVE

Lyric by HAL DAVID
Music by BURT BACHARACH

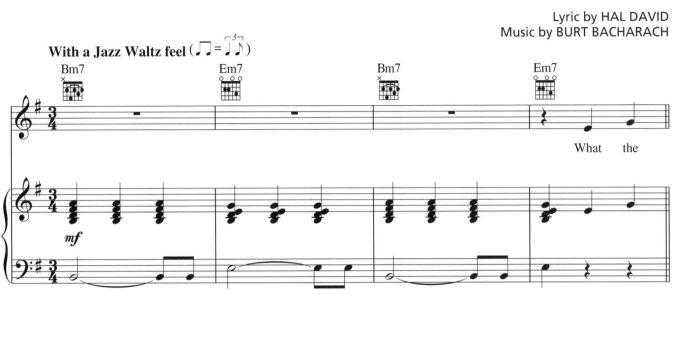

THE TWIST

Words and Music by
HANK BALLARD

UP ON THE ROOF

Words and Music by GERRY GOFFIN
and CAROLE KING

UP, UP AND AWAY

Words and Music by
JIMMY WEBB

WALK ON BY

Lyric by HAL DAVID
Music by BURT BACHARACH

WICHITA LINEMAN

Words and Music by
JIMMY WEBB

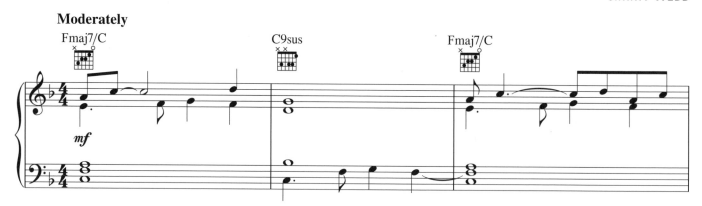

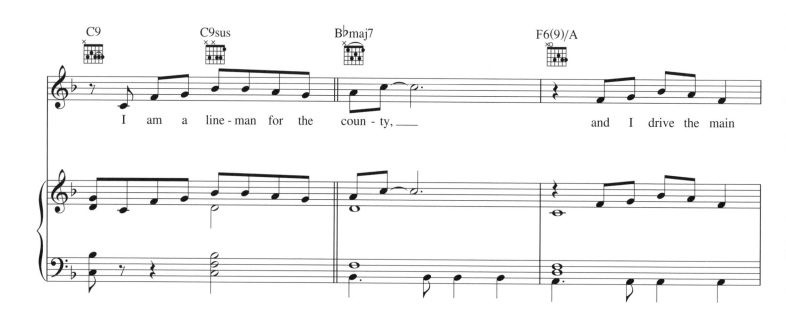

WILD THING

Words and Music by
CHIP TAYLOR

Moderately slow, with a beat

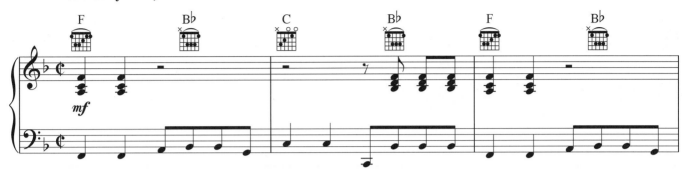

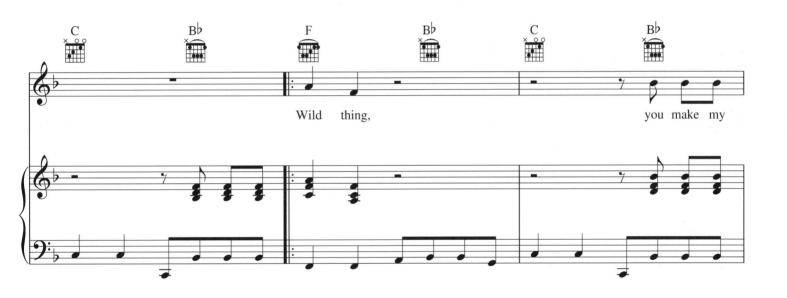

Wild thing, you make my

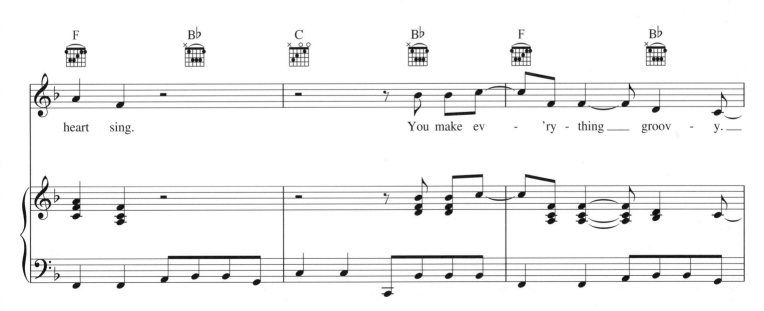

heart sing. You make ev - 'ry - thing___ groov - y.___

Wild thing.

Wild thing, I _____ think I love you.
Wild thing, I _____ think you move me.

But I wan-na know _

_____ for sure.
_____ for sure.

Come on and hold me tight. _
Come on and hold me tight. _

I love you.
You move me.

WOOLY BULLY

Words and Music by
DOMINGO SAMUDIO

Moderately

Mat - ty told Hat - ty _____ a - bout a
Hat - ty told Mat - ty, _____ "Let's don't
Mat - ty told Hat - ty, _____ "That's the

thing she saw. ___ Had two big horns ___
take no chance. ___ Let's not be L sev - en.
thing to do. ___ Get yo' some - one real - ly

and a wool - y jaw. ___ Wool - y
Come and learn to dance." ___
to pull the wool with you." ___

WOULDN'T IT BE NICE

Words by and Music by BRIAN WILSON,
TONY ASHER and MIKE LOVE

Would-n't it be nice if we were old- er, ___ then ___ we would-n't
nice if we could wake ___ up ___ in ___ the morn-ing

have to wait ___ so ___ long ___ and would-n't it be nice to live to-geth-
when the day ___ is ___ new ___ and af-ter that to spend the day to-geth-

-er ___ in ___ the kind of world where we'd ___ be - long. ___
-er, ___ hold ___ each oth - er close the whole ___ night ___ through. ___

YOU'VE MADE ME SO VERY HAPPY

Words and Music by BERRY GORDY, FRANK E. WILSON,
BRENDA HOLLOWAY and PATRICE HOLLOWAY

Moderately

YELLOW SUBMARINE

Words and Music by JOHN LENNON
and PAUL McCARTNEY

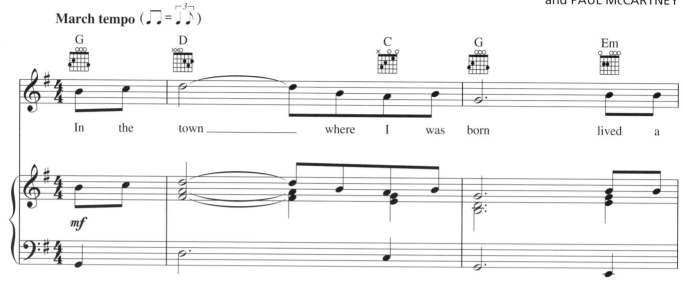

YOU'VE LOST THAT LOVIN' FEELIN'

Words and Music by BARRY MANN,
CYNTHIA WEIL and PHIL SPECTOR

close your eyes ___ an-y-more when I kiss your lips. ___
wel-come look ___ in your eyes when I reach for you. ___

And there's no ten-der-ness ___ like be-fore in your fin-ger-tips.
And, girl, you're start-ing to ___ crit-i-cize lit-tle things ___ I do.

HAL•LEONARD ESSENTIAL SONGS

Play the best songs from the Roaring '20s to today! Each collection features dozens of the most memorable songs of each decade, or in your favorite musical style, arranged in piano/vocal/guitar format.

THE 1920s

Over 100 songs that shaped the decade: Ain't We Got Fun? • Basin Street Blues • Bye Bye Blackbird • Can't Help Lovin' Dat Man • I Wanna Be Loved by You • Makin' Whoopee • Ol' Man River • Puttin' On the Ritz • Toot, Toot, Tootsie • Yes Sir, That's My Baby • and more.
00311200..............................$24.95

THE 1930s

97 essential songs from the 1930s: April in Paris • Body and Soul • Cheek to Cheek • Falling in Love with Love • Georgia on My Mind • Heart and Soul • I'll Be Seeing You • The Lady Is a Tramp • Mood Indigo • My Funny Valentine • You Are My Sunshine • and more.
00311193..............................$24.95

THE 1940s

An amazing collection of over 100 songs from the '40s: Boogie Woogie Bugle Boy • Don't Get Around Much Anymore • Have I Told You Lately That I Love You • I'll Remember April • Route 66 • Sentimental Journey • Take the "A" Train • You'd Be So Nice to Come Home To • and more.
00311192..............................$24.95

THE 1950s

Over 100 pivotal songs from the 1950s, including: All Shook Up • Bye Bye Love • Chantilly Lace • Fever • Great Balls of Fire • Kansas City • Love and Marriage • Mister Sandman • Rock Around the Clock • Sixteen Tons • Tennessee Waltz • Wonderful! Wonderful! • and more.
00311191..............................$24.95

THE 1960s

104 '60s essentials, including: Baby Love • California Girls • Dancing in the Street • Hey Jude • I Heard It Through the Grapevine • Respect • Stand by Me • Twist and Shout • Will You Love Me Tomorrow • Yesterday • You Keep Me Hangin' On • and more.
00311190..............................$24.95

Prices, contents and availability subject to change without notice.

THE 1970s

Over 80 of the best songs from the '70s: American Pie • Band on the Run • Come Sail Away • Dust in the Wind • I Feel the Earth Move • Let It Be • Morning Has Broken • Smoke on the Water • Take a Chance on Me • The Way We Were • You're So Vain • and more.
00311189........................$24.95

THE 1980s

Over 70 classics from the age of power pop and hair metal: Against All Odds • Call Me • Ebony and Ivory • The Heat Is On • Jump • Manic Monday • Sister Christian • Time After Time • Up Where We Belong • What's Love Got to Do with It • and more.
00311188 ....$24.95

THE 1990s

68 songs featuring country-crossover, swing revival, the birth of grunge, and more: Change the World • Fields of Gold • Ironic • Livin' La Vida Loca • More Than Words • Smells like Teen Spirit • Walking in Memphis • Zoot Suit Riot • and more.
00311187 ....$24.95

THE 2000s

59 of the best songs that brought in the new millennium: Accidentally in Love • Beautiful • Don't Know Why • Get the Party Started • Hey Ya! • I Hope You Dance • 1985 • This Love • A Thousand Miles • Wherever You Will Go • Who Let the Dogs Out • You Raise Me Up • and more.
00311186..............................$24.95

BROADWAY

Over 90 songs of the stage: Any Dream Will Do • Blue Skies • Cabaret • Don't Cry for Me, Argentina • Edelweiss • Hello, Dolly! • I'll Be Seeing You • Memory • The Music of the Night • Oklahoma • Summer Nights • There's No Business Like Show Business • Tomorrow • more.
00311222..............................$24.95

CHRISTMAS

Over 100 essential holiday favorites: Blue Christmas • The Christmas Song • Deck the Hall • Frosty the Snow Man • Joy to the World • Merry Christmas, Darling • Rudolph the Red-Nosed Reindeer • Silver Bells • and more!
00311241 ....$24.95

JAZZ STANDARDS

99 jazz classics no music library should be without: Autumn in New York • Body and Soul • Don't Get Around Much Anymore • Easy to Love (You'd Be So Easy to Love) • I've Got You Under My Skin • The Lady Is a Tramp • Mona Lisa • Satin Doll • Stardust • Witchcraft • and more.
00311226 ....$24.95

LOVE SONGS

Over 80 romantic hits: Can You Feel the Love Tonight • Endless Love • From This Moment On • Have I Told You Lately • I Just Called to Say I Love You • Love Will Keep Us Together • My Heart Will Go On • Wonderful Tonight • You Are So Beautiful • more.
00311235 ....$24.95

MOVIE SONGS

94 of the most popular silver screen songs: Alfie • Beauty and the Beast • Chariots of Fire • Footloose • I Will Remember You • Jailhouse Rock • Moon River • People • Somewhere Out There • Summer Nights • Unchained Melody • and more.
00311236 ....$24.95

TV SONGS

Over 100 terrific tube tunes, including: The Addams Family Theme • Bonanza • The Brady Bunch • Desperate Housewives Main Title • I Love Lucy • Law and Order • Linus and Lucy • Sesame Street Theme • Theme from the Simpsons • Theme from the X-Files • and more!
00311223 ....$24.95

FOR MORE INFORMATION, SEE YOUR LOCAL MUSIC DEALER,
OR WRITE TO:

HAL•LEONARD® CORPORATION

7777 W. BLUEMOUND RD. P.O. BOX 13819 MILWAUKEE, WI 53213

Complete contents listings are available online at **www.halleonard.com**

0805